Amazing Graces

An uncommon book of prayers

Thankyou for your contribution.
Ken Cooper

Contents

3	**I**ntroduction
10	**B**usiness
14	**F**ellowship
17	**C**ommunity
21	**I**nternational
24	**V**ocational
29	**G**uest Speakers
35	**O**ther Meetings
41	**S**pecial Graces
47	**R**eferences
48	**N**otes

Introduction

These prayers are the result of gathering together the graces that have been offered by the presidents of the Rotary Club of Coventry Breakfast for a number of years. Over this period this Club has been engaged in international fundraising activities that have led to a close relationship with ITDG.

Rotary meetings are usually held weekly and generally start with a grace. The Coventry Breakfast graces have been written to introduce the topic of each meeting in a thought provoking way. A religious person may find a deep meaning within, a non-religious person may be made to ponder the words, while both may enjoy an underlying humour that is often generated by the rhymes.

Should a major event occur which requires a straightforward thought of support and comfort a suitable grace has generally been adapted and these are also included.

These graces have become part of the Rotary Club of Coventry Breakfast tradition, and a groan or lively comment often follows them. Rotarians are part of the general public who give their service in support of the local and wider

communities. The layout of this book reflects the way that the Rotary meetings are organised, the range of service activities and therefore represents a natural and ready reference.

With several years of material to build on, this book is seen as a first volume, with the potential for many more as graces continue to be written. The profits will be equally shared between ITDG and the Rotary Club of Coventry Breakfast. The sustainability of *"practical answers to poverty"* (ITDG) combines with the international outreach of *"service above self"* (Rotary) to provide an effective ongoing means of support for those in need worldwide.

These graces are offered to the reader and to Rotary Clubs in the hope that they will not only provide a useful reference for graces at other Rotary meetings or similar gatherings, but also be of interest, inspiration, and enjoyment to all.

ITDG

ITDG is an international non-governmental development organisation and a British registered charity. Through its practical project work, ITDG is involved

at all stages of helping small-scale producers to develop, adapt and share technical knowledge, experience and skills.

Almost all the technology being developed today is designed to meet the demands of industrialised countries. Much of this technology cannot be used by the majority of the world's population because of its cost or complexity. ITDG recognises this and aims to reflect the needs of people in poverty in all its projects by providing appropriate and sustainable technology options.

Through ITDG, people can develop technology that puts the user first:
- Technology that draws on their experience, and feeds it
- That recognises their potential, and releases it
- That respects their environment and nurtures it
- That builds on their past to sustain the future.

Founded in 1966 on the thinking of Dr E F Schumacher and his book, "Small is Beautiful", ITDG has always sought to find practical answers to poverty through appropriate technology. Its work is currently focused in Bangladesh, Kenya, Nepal, Peru, Sri Lanka, Sudan and Zimbabwe. It has two subsidiary companies, one a consultancy called ITC and one based in London, ITDG Publishing.

ITDG enjoys strong links with Rotary and has provided considerable support to this book. The net proceeds are being shared between the International Committee of the Breakfast Club, Rotary Foundation, and Marginal Farmers projects in Kenya, for which they will provide matching funds.

Rotary Club of Coventry Breakfast

The Rotary Club of Coventry Breakfast is a dual gender Rotary Club, chartered in 1992, situated in the City of Coventry in the West Midlands metropolitan county in the United Kingdom. There are five Rotary Clubs in the City (Coventry, Coventry North, Coventry Jubilee, Coventry Phoenix and Coventry Breakfast) and one Rotaract Club (Coventry Jubilee).

Our District, 1060, is in the heart of England and covers the West Midlands, Warwickshire and parts of Shropshire and Worcestershire and currently contains some seventy Rotary Clubs.

Coventry Breakfast has undertaken several significant service projects in the relatively short period since its inception. Some examples of these are:

- Collection of over twelve thousand spectacles for Vision Aid Overseas (in just three years);

- Establishment of a water supply project in Kenya;
- Support of various charities such as Friends in the West, Hope and Homes for Children, and Water Aid.

However, the essential spirit of the Club is based on fellowship, humour and good friendship. This is reflected in members giving their time and energies in joining with Rotary Clubs, Rotaract and other service organisations in local Community and Vocational projects and social activities.

For further information concerning ITDG and the Rotary Club of Coventry Breakfast activities, see References at the back of this book.

Enjoy ...

We're grateful Lord for every day For it's true what they say, That when we all to Thee do pray Thou wilt reveal the perfect WAY.

Business

Business Meeting 1

Father bless today our business,

Please make it good and lasting;

And when we come to eat our meal

We thank Thee we're not fasting!

Business Meeting 2

Bless this Thy Friday morning

O God of all the earth;

And let the business meeting

Prove what we all are worth!

Business Meeting 3

We have this business meeting,

Summer's here! We shan't need heating:

Dear Father please bless all those here

This lovely day so fine and ... nice?

Business Meeting 4

> **F**or what we do receive,
>
> Lord help us to believe
>
> That there is plenty more
>
> In your eternal store.

Business Meeting 5

> **F**or what we are about to receive,
>
> Please make us truly glad;
>
> And with our plans help us to 'sieve'
>
> The good from very bad.

Business Meeting 6

> **W**e thank Thee our dear Father
>
> For everything Thou dost,
>
> Please guide our business plans today
>
> So they don't gather rust!

Business Meeting 7

> **L**et's start with this simple greeting,
>
> Praise the lovely business meeting.
>
> Thank you Lord for all our skill,
>
> Finely tuned to do Thy will;
>
> Helping us to help each other,
>
> Treating all as friend and brother.

Business Meeting 8

> **T**hank you Father for this meeting,
>
> Help us run it without bleating;
>
> And teach us too, to ask not beg,
>
> and give one's friend the last fried egg.

Dear Lord and Father of us all,
The big, the thin, the high, the small,
Keep us oiled and running smooth
Like an engine in its groove,
All parts working as a team;
Together reach the Rotary dream!

 *Fellowship*

Fellowship 1

Jack and Jill went up the hill

To fetch a pail of water;

Jack tripped up and broke his cup

And Jill cracked up with laughter.

We're grateful Lord, when times are hard,

You've given everyone

The priceless thing that heals our ills,

The timeless gift of fun!

Fellowship 2

We thank Thee Lord for Friday

And for our fellowship,

We thank Thee for the friends we have …

… (four seconds) … (That's it!)

Fellowship 3

We thank Thee Lord, for what you are,

And everything you be,

We Thank Thee for us being here,

For coffee and warm/hot? tea ...

Fellowship 4

We thank Thee for this meeting,

For those with various means,

For all our food and fellowship,

For eggs and toast and ... orange juice.

Fellowship 5

We thank you for our fellowship,

In friendship serving Thee,

We thank Thee for our breakfast,

But note that Friendship's free!

Protect Thy children everywhere No matter where they be, And let our lives express Thy care In love and constancy.

 Community

Charity, giving of cheques

    Dear Lord please help us to believe

    It's good to both give and receive;

    For we are richer when we part

    With off'rings from within the heart,

    And thanking Thee for what is given,

    Leads us nearer, Lord, to heaven.

Community Fellowship 1

    We thank Thee for the fellowship

    That we have come to share,

    For all things that you give us,

    From food and clothes to wear.

    We thank Thee for Community,

    They are a lovely bunch,

    And we look forward to their show

    This breakfast, not this lunch!

Community Fellowship 2

    We give our thanks for Community

    Their simple faith and humility.

    May we like them be straight and true

    And work for others, and for you.

Community Fellowship 3

    Dear Lord, it's community time,

    And we rejoice in simple rhyme.

    For when we do what must be done

    We know that we'll all enjoy the meeting.

Care in the Community

    Lord, please make us all aware

    That Thy Love gives us constant care;

    Help us then to love each other,

    Holding hands as sister, brother.

Community Meeting

We thank Thee Father of all things

For friendship and for unity;

let's all rejoice that everyone

Is part of ONE community!

Community Fellowship 4

We thank Thee for Community,

And all that it does bring.

It makes us want to laugh AND SHOUT,

It makes us want to sing.

We thank Thee Lord especial-ly

On this chil-ly cold morn-ing!

Community Fellowship 5

We give thanks where'er we be

For having our community,

For the great gift of fellowship

Makes coming here a worthwhile visit.

Dear Lord who reigns North, East, West, South,

We thank Thee that we have a mouth!

It's useful when you want to sigh (say)

Hi there Pommies, and Good Dye (day).

International

International Fellowship 1

Help us to recognise that God is international;

He is no respecter of persons, race or creed;

His love knows no boundaries.

International Fellowship 2

Dear Lord,

We are grateful for International Fellowship.

(Complaint the previous week's grace was too long!)

Charity walk up Kilimanjaro (Trevor)

Dear Lord we praise Thee as the fount

Of things that last for ever:

We thank Thee that upon the mount

You took good care of Trevor!

International Fellowship 3

    We give Thee thanks across the world

    As Your great wisdom is unfurled;

    It speaks of peace to son and daughter,

    It helps us do just what we ought'a.

International Fellowship 4

    For this international meeting

    We give thanks to Thee our Lord,

    Confident that with our colleagues

    No one here will be ignored!

Lahiru Perera, Country Director ITDG charity

    We welcome those from far abroad

    It's really good to see you,

    And we thank God for all they've done,

    Especially LAHIRU.

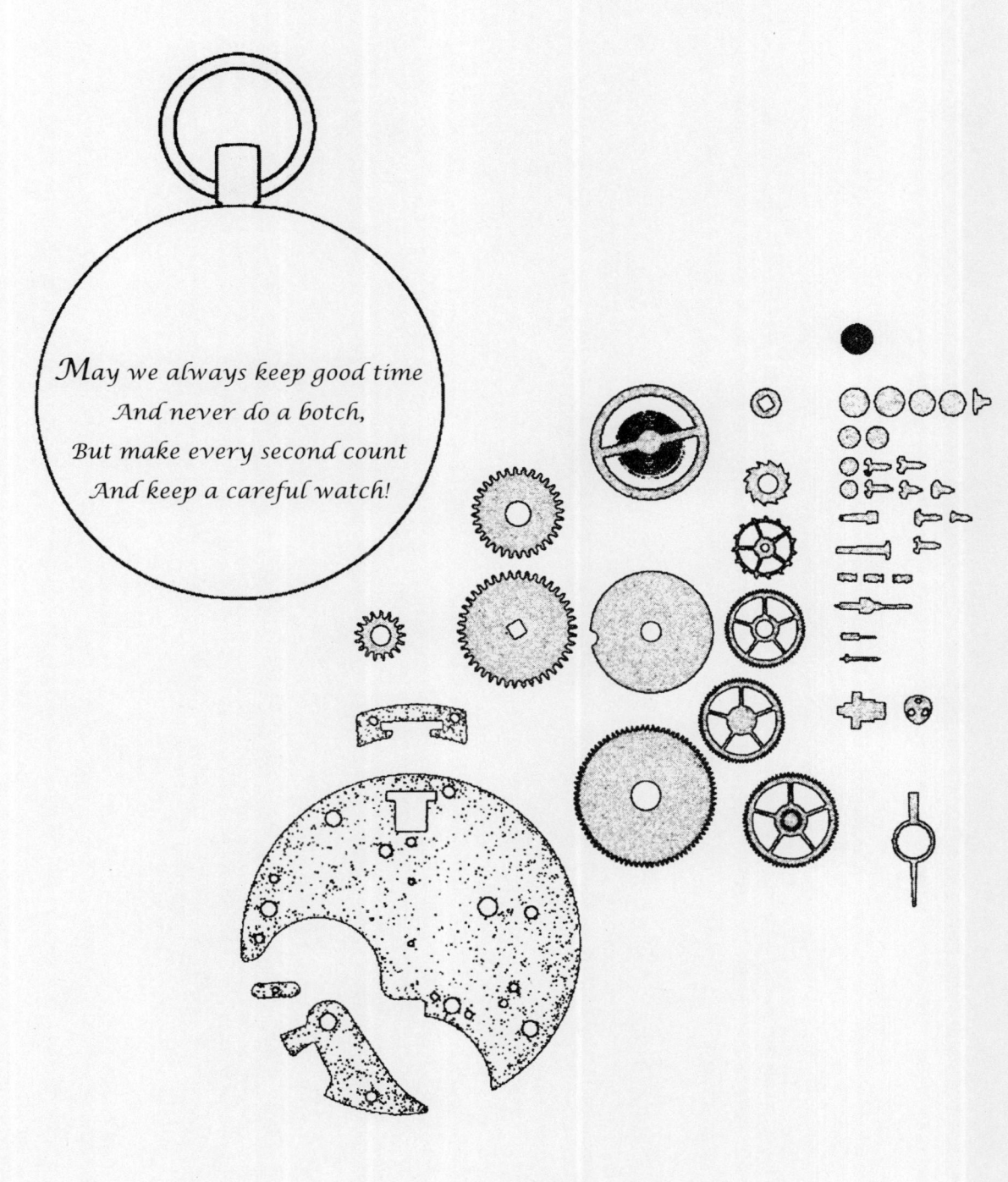

Vocational

Crime prevention

    We pray for those who, in detention,

    Had not the help of crime prevention.

    Grant us Lord we help pre-empt

    All situations that may tempt!

Exchange student from Nashville (first visit)

    We thank Thee Lord for this exchange

    Far from our Coventree (Coventry),

    Across the hills and mountain range

    From state of Tennessee.

    Please bless Lord all those who speak

    And bless the ending of this week.

Zimbabwean student training for law

Soaring, Lord, with wings of eagle,

Comes our Sophie, learning legal:

Grant her strength to so fulfill

The inner joy: to do Thy will!

So, dear Father, give us grace,

To support the human race,

Standing firm to uphold law,

Rich in spirit, no one is poor!

Exchange: Australian

Dear Lord who reigns North, East, West, South,

We thank Thee that we have a mouth!

It's useful when you want to sigh (say)

Hi there Pommies, and Good Dye (day).

Clocks and Watches Museum

      May we always keep good time

      And never do a botch,

      But make every second count

      And keep a careful watch!

Exchange: Youth

      Help us to see it is not strange

      To offer things in fair exchange.

      So bless all those beneath this roof,

      The middle aged, the old, the youth!

The Coventry Way (Coventry Footpath)

      We're grateful Lord for every day

      For it's true just what they say,

      That when we all to Thee do pray

      Thou wilt reveal the perfect WAY.

Job talk

We thank thee Lord for what we do

The way we are employed,

The knowledge that if we are true

We will be overjoyed;

And we pray no one will walk

When Alan gives us his job talk.

Exchange student from Nashville

Dear Lord we seek to do Thy will

Wherever we may be:

From here at home or in Nashville

That's far off Tennessee!

We thank Thee that you let life fizz,

We thank Thee for Colleen;

Please give us answers to her quiz,

And bless the British Queen.

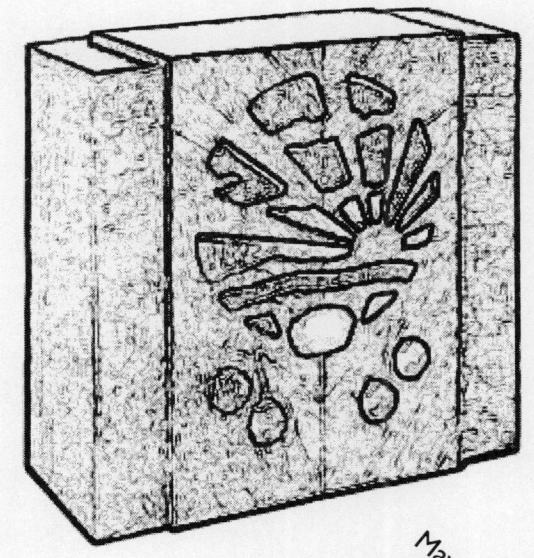

Dear Lord we thank Thee for our media

E'en those, like us, who come and feedy 'ere!

Enhanced with song and chat that's broad-cast

May all who hear enjoy their break-fast.

Guest Speakers

Bee Keepers' Association (first flight)

>Dear Lord we thank Thee for the BEE,
>
>It is a little treasure;
>
>It brings to life a lot of BUZZ
>
>And fills our lives with pleasure!

Coventry Rotary History

>Dear Lord, as life is such a mystery
>
>Help us to learn things from the past.
>
>Hide not from us those bits of history
>
>On which our present has been cast.
>
>Help us to learn 'bout Rotary
>
>And those who come from Coventry.

Coventry History part 1

We thank Thee for our glorious past

From which our present has been cast;

Grant us Lord that we have fun

With Hist'ry Lesson – Part One!

Coventry History part 2

With more history now unfurled

We see our place within the world.

Stand fast, friends, in Coventry blue

United in the things we do:

We thank Thee Father for part 2.

Children Homes in Need

Protect Thy children everywhere

No matter where they be,

And let out lives express Thy care

In love and constancy.

Festival of Light

We thank Thee Lord that day through night

Thy goodness stays the same;

And with these words "Let there be light"

We glory in Thy name.

Friends of the West

Dear Lord we know that you know best

And in Thy Love we can find rest;

For all you do we're truly blest,

Including all Friends of the West.

Refugees in Coventry, UK

Dear Lord please help us to see

The plight of every refugee,

Help us remove from this world strife

And give to all a better life.

Local radio: Job talk by mining specialist

>**D**ear Lord we thank Thee for our media
>
>E'en those, like us, who come and feedy 'ere!
>
>Enhanced with song and chat that's broad-cast
>
>May all who hear enjoy their break-fast.
>
>Dear Lord please also bless our John
>
>A mine of in-for-ma-tion!

Retina Pigmentosa Society

>**M**ay all those with failing sight
>
>Sense the presence of Thy might;
>
>Send Thy love to mend and heal
>
>That each Thy tender touch may feel.

Uganda Medical Centre for Children (Africa Choir)

>Dear Lord may we all sing Thy praise
>
>And recognise Thy glory,
>
>So that the children that You raise
>
>Can share in love this story:
>
>That all who seek in Thee their wealth
>
>May bear witness to good health.

Bee Keepers' Association (second flight)

>Dear Lord we thank Thee for the bee
>
>It is a little treasure,
>
>It fills our lives with lots of buzz
>
>And gives us lots of pleasure!
>
>And so I say as your Queen Bee
>
>A-standing by my throne,
>
>I'm grateful for all you out there
>
>For each and every drone!

Dear Lord we thank Thee for the BEE, It is a little treasure; It brings to life a lot of BUZZ And fills our lives with pleasure! Dear Lord we thank Thee for the BEE, It is a little treasure; It brings to life a lot of BUZZ And fills our lives with pleasure!

Other Meetings

A welcome start

> **D**ear Lord, help us to do our best
> And make each welcome as a guest:
> Notwithstanding race or creed,
> Help us to meet a brother's need.

A welcome to friends overseas

> **W**e thank Thee Lord for fellowship,
> It is a lovely thing;
> It makes us want to laugh and shout,
> It makes us want to sing!
> We're grateful Lord for Your outreach
> Across the waters blue,
> For sending guests from far off lands,
> Sri Lanka, Nepal, Peru!

Club Meeting

> **W**e Thank Thee for what matters most,
>
> A selfless friendly club;
>
> And lots of marmalade and toast,
>
> And lots of lovely... other things!

Club Service

> **F**or what we have received
>
> We give Thee thanks;
>
> For what we have achieved
>
> We give Thee praise;
>
> For what is still to be done
>
> We seek Thy strength and guidance.

Annual dinner, magician cabaret

> **D**ear Lord it really would be tragic,
>
> If in our lives there was no magic;
>
> So let us thank you for this gift
>
> That gives to all an instant lift.

Special Meeting: Election (US Presidential wrangling!)

    Dear Lord we ask that You take note

    That now <u>we</u> gotta take a vote!

    Grant us that there's no derision

    And give us please a clear decision!

Special Meeting – election

    Dear Lord please bless this special meeting.

    Help us gathered here select

    Those worthy to hold fast this greeting:

    "We serve the World"; please so elect.

District Governor speaker

    We thank Thee Lord for our DG

    Especially as its him not me:

    Please give your wisdom to us all

    That we may learn to walk not crawl.

Charity, giving of cheques

>Dear Lord please help us to believe
>
>It's good to both give and receive,
>
>For we are richer when we part
>
>With off'rings from within the heart;
>
>And thanking Thee for what is given,
>
>Lead us nearer, Lord, to heaven.

District Governor (who likes steam trains!)

>Dear Lord and Father of us all,
>
>The big, the thin, the high, the small,
>
>Keep us oiled and running smooth
>
>Like an engine in its groove,
>
>All parts working as a team;
>
>Together reach the Rotary dream!

Club Assembly

We welcome all at this our Club

Assembled here for friendly grub!

And so because we're never bored

We give thanks to Thee our Lord.

Handover

The year has been and gone, – it's went:

We'll soon have 'nother president!

And if this makes you feel quite chary,

Worry not, her name is Mary!

And so our thanks for all things new,

Each day, each life, the things we'll do.

Help us also have good times,

Protect us from excessive fines!

We thank Thee Lord for this our Club:

Now form a queue and get your grub!

THE YEAR HAS BEEN AND GONE, -IT'S WENT:
WE'LL SOON HAVE 'NOTHER PRESIDENT!
AND IF THIS MAKES YOU FEEL QUITE CHARY,
WORRY NOT, HER NAME IS MARY!
AND SO OUR THANKS FOR ALL THINGS NEW,
EACH DAY, EACH LIFE, THE THINGS WE'LL DO.
HELP US ALSO HAVE GOOD TIMES,
PROTECT US FROM EXCESSIVE FINES!
WE THANK THEE LORD FOR THIS OUR CLUB:
NOW FORM A QUEUE AND GET YOUR GRUB!

Isis ... the greatest of the Egyptian goddesses and possessed of immense magical powers. Isis is the divine mother and protector.

Special Graces

In memory of Diana, Princess of Wales

> **F**or this our International Fellowship,
>
> We bow our heads in memory of Diana,
>
> Knowing that, as we celebrate her life,
>
> Our gratitude is best shown by doing
>
> Both the grand and little things that help others.

Millennium Christmas

> **W**ith this our last meeting of the 20th Century,
>
> grant us O Lord the same faith you gave Abraham
>
> nearly 2000 years BC, that whereas he founded
>
> a nation, that we may go forward and make one
>
> nation of the world.

Christmas

Dear Lord, in this Christmas season, please give us the grace to remember those less fortunate than ourselves.
May all feel the touch of Thy love, finding therein peace and true friendship.

New Year

This is a grace that's just for us
Excluding those that missed the bus!
At the start of this New Year
We hold our fellowship quite dear;
We thank Thee Father for good friends,
For Rotary that never ends!

Worst floods in 50 years

>Dear Lord, we offer our prayers of support
>to all those who are suffering from the
>effects of floods or other personal disasters.
>May Thy love reach them, support them,
>and provide them with all they need.

Aberfan remembered – 35th anniversary

>Let all those present that now can
>Recall the horror: Aberfan.
>The feeling of sheer disbelief,
>The local pain, the national grief.
>But rising from emotions deep
>Eternal hope began to creep, –
>Hand to hand and heart to heart
>True brotherhood did play its part.
>We give thanks for courage strong
>That ensures that life goes on.

First millennium meeting

>AD 2000 it has come
>
>Let's all rejoice together,
>
>And thank Thee Lord for all you've done
>
>For life, for love, for weather!

Foot and Mouth epidemic

>Dear Lord, we offer our prayers of support
>to all those who are affected by the present crisis
>in the countryside. May all unite in the bond of
>togetherness, knowing that true friendship
>is indeed Service Before Self.

Terrorist acts in America 11 September 2001

>Dear Father, in the aftermath of terror, may we
>still feel Thy Love, reaching and touching all hearts,
>supporting those in need, replacing hurt with
>healing, anger with wisdom, and revealing the true
>brotherhood of all nations and peoples.

We thank Thee Lord for all Thou art And for the gift of love: May we, through Thee, lift ev'ry heart With strength that's from above!

... **E**nd?

References

ITDG Limited
Charity Commission Registration No. 247257
Company Registration No. 871954 England
The Schumacher Centre
Bourton Hall, Bourton-on-Dunsmore
Rugby, Warwickshire, UK. CV23 9QZ
http://www.oneworld.org/itdg

Rotary Club of Coventry Breakfast
Charity Commission Registration No. 1071587
Contact us via our Website:
http://www.coventrybreakfastrotary.org.uk
or email at:
Contact@coventrybreakfastrotary.org.uk.

First published by ITDG Limited and Rotary Club of Coventry Breakfast
UK March 2002

Copyright © 2002 Rotary Club of Coventry Breakfast
Written by Ken Cooper
Designed by Jim Jobson

Printed by IPH Litho (Coventry) Limited
Church Lawford, Rugby, Warwickshire, UK

ISBN 0-903031-01-9